WHAT COULD HAVE

ENDED

MY LIFE

CHANGED

MY LIFE

THE AUTOBIOGRAPHY OF
DECARLO CORNISH

What Could Have Ended My Life Changed My Life
The Autobiography of Decarlo Cornish

ISBN 978-1-947741-48-5

Book published by:

Kingdom Publishing LLC
Odenton, MD 21113

First printed in the U.S.A.

Dedication

I would like to dedicate this book to everyone who is currently in the street life, who think it's there only option. I wrote this book showing you what I went through so you will not have to go through the same struggle.

I also dedicate this book to my two sons, Amir and Armon, who while I was on the ground filled with blood and holes in my body, gave me a reason to not give up. I'm living proof that it's never too late to change your life.

I also want to dedicate this book to Javante Parker, Teddy Scurry, and Shaun Crowdy who lost their lives to the struggle of the streets.

Acknowledgements

I would like to acknowledge first and foremost, God, for giving me the strength to survive and be able to write this book.

I would like to send a special thanks to the University of Maryland Shock Trauma medical staff for keeping me alive after two near-death experiences with gun shots.

I would like to thank all my family and friends who kept me in their prayers.

Birth & Early Childhood
1991-2002

It was 11:30am. My mother was leaving her brothers funeral and headed to Anne Arundel General Hospital in Annapolis, Maryland to give birth to me. During the laboring process, my mother's body was in distress. She was too young and underweight to handle the pregnancy and ultimately, she was dying. When the doctor's asked her who's life she wanted to save, she chose mine. My mother ended up passing away in the process of delivering me. After the doctors cut open her stomach and took me from my mother's womb, they were able to bring her back to life. It was only by the grace of God my mother's life was saved and a star was born.

My brothers and I went to stay with my grandfather in the back of Arwell, while my mother turned to the streets and drug game. Arwell is one of the roughest neighborhoods in Pioneer City. Although the community was small, there was a lot going on that I witnessed as a child. Growing up in the back of Arwell was traumatizing. If you weren't from Arwell or living that "tough" lifestyle it was rough. You would get picked with all the time for not belonging. Every other day somebody was either fighting, getting robbed, or getting shot. Kids would ride up and down the street or run around and play. The dope boys would stand outside on the corner and hang around; police riding up and down the street cracking heads and walking in and out of the alley.

I lived with my grandfather for most of my childhood. My mother was living her life in the streets at the time and didn't want to risk my brothers and I being around if someone tried to run up in the house and rob it or if the police decided to bust in. I remember being a toddler about 3 years old living back in Arwell. My middle brother had just been born and was only a couple of months old. My mother was getting out of the hospital after being in there 5-7 days from having my brother. It just so happens that my cousin's lady had me with her over her house that day. My mother was dealing with my brothers' father. He was a good, low key person who stayed getting money and was never flashy about it. I remember when he bought this blue Porsche with the Gold BBS. He would come and pick us up in it all the time.

I was just a toddler that day back at the house. My mother and little brother were both in the house when some people came in to try and rob my brother's father. I remember one of the them came through the storm window and opened the door to let the other's in that were with him. As soon as my mother heard them downstairs, she ran to the closet to get the gun. They shot one time through the house. My little brother was in his bassinet the whole time this was going on and he never woke up. He slept through all of it. I was glad that he was good through it all, because it could have been a lot worse.

Growing up in my grandfather's 3-bedroom house wasn't the best experience especially because all the boys had to share one room. My two brothers, two uncles and myself had bunkbeds and slept two to a bed. We had toys and video games but we it seemed like we stayed on punishment; mostly for stuff like fighting each other, sneaking outside, getting put off the Sunday activity church bus and being suspended from school. I was the main one getting beatings from my grandfather because I would get suspended from elementary school almost every other week. My two aunts slept in the other room and then their mother and my grandfather had their room. My grandfather did his best to keep food on the table and provide for all seven of us. He retired from the army and began working at the Naval Academy. He would always bring food home every day and make sure the refrigerator and freezer stayed full. The problem was we had an infestation of roaches. They would be all over the place, in the cabinets, on the dishes, in the refrigerator crawling all over the food. I remember having to shake my clothes off every day before school and check my bookbag to make sure they weren't in there. It was crazy having to wake up every day or sometimes in the middle of the night to roaches crawling on you. My grandfather had the house bombed so many times but somehow, they would find their way back. After a while, I just got used to living with them.

Granddad's house was always the spot for all my cousins to come over and chill. We were always having cookouts and playing spades. Grandad's friends would come over and play horse-shoes, have gambling parties, dice games and Tunk matches. Most of the time after school we would be in the field playing throw up tackle or in the woods playing on the train tracks. Sometimes I would get on a bike and ride around looking for some trouble to get into. Since our parents never bought us bikes, we would ride out to the nice communities outside of our neighborhood and steal bikes. We knew we would always come across expensive trick bikes or mountain bikes outside of our community. I would even steal bikes from the kids that lived next door or up the street from us. It really didn't matter who it was as long as they had a bike I could steal. The neighbor kids and I would fight over the bikes but we would be back hanging out with each other the next day.

One day I was walking out of the house and I see this dude running from the back of the houses. It looked like he was coming from Richfield running towards Arwell. He looked like he was running as though someone was chasing him. When I saw who it was running, I knew he had just robbed someone. Before he hit the street, the person chasing him bent the corner with his arm stretched out pointing his gun at his back. All you hear is boom, boom, boom, boom and he hit the ground. A lady came running out of the house to help him. This was my first time ever seeing something like that at such a young age. I would see it on TV all the time but seeing it in real life gave me a different feeling. I knew this wouldn't be my last time seeing something like that happen. I experienced way too much living in that neighborhood, from drugs to guns, police beating the dope boys up and dog fights. My elementary school was right up the street across from the front store and I would walk there every day. I remember walking to the front store every day. One day I saw a body just leaning over the fence out back of the store. At first, I thought I was seeing things but when I looked down there was big puddle of blood in the grass where the body was hanging. I couldn't believe what I was seeing. I had just seen this man standing outside of the store the day before. I just shook my head and kept walking to school.

I looked forward to going to school every day because I knew I was going to come home with something new that I took from somebody or from the principal's office. I would come home with Pokemon cards, Yo-Yo's, money, phones, etc. This was all stuff that I didn't have back at home. I could have easily asked my mother to buy these things, but I would of rather stole them. I used to hate when the book fair would come around because all the other kids would come to school with money to get a book, but I never had any to spend. It wasn't like I couldn't get the money if I had asked, I just never felt like asking, so I would just take matters into my own hands and steal the books so that I wouldn't feel left out. I didn't want to put too much on my mom anyways. She already had enough going on as a single mother trying to raise three boys; I knew it wasn't east for her. I wasn't proud of myself for what I was doing, and I knew it wasn't cool. I knew if my mother would have found out she would have been mad and gave me a beating. All I had to do was ask her or my cousin Carlus for something I wanted and they would have made sure I got it.

I couldn't wait for school to let out so that I could walk across the street to the corner store. All the hustlers would hang out in front of the store JJ's Pizza waiting on their chicken boxes or whatever they ordered. They would play the Pac-man game inside and talk and mess around with the females that pulled up to the store. I was all the hustler's favorite little kid and I was the worst kid out there. I always hit their pockets for a dollar before it was time for me to go home. I would always walk home with at least $5 since most of them ended up giving me more than a dollar. I couldn't' wait to get home and add whatever money I got to my stash box. My house was right behind the corner store and when school got out at 3:15pm, I wouldn't get home until 4:30 or 5 o clock. I was always being punished for something I was doing in school or for hanging on the corner with the dope boys, so my mindset was to stay out as long as I can before my mother gets home.

When I was able to go outside, I would go to my man Dexter's house. He lived down the street in Arwell. We would play basketball in his backyard or I would go to the playground out front of my house where most of the older people would hang out at. I used to go to the barber shop called C-More Jazz on 175. Earl was my barber. Sometimes I would sit there until my mother was finished getting her hair done. My mother would see Ms. Tracey to do her hair, and still to this day, she goes to her. I always wanted something to eat from this carryout place out back called Mona's. I would always get the Chicken box from there. Ms. Mona was a very nice lady, and everybody would show her love and eat there. Her business is still up and running to this day. She has a bigger store up the street from where her old store was.

On some nice, summer days my mother would could get us and take us to Annapolis gardens; they call it "da onion." That was the hood for real. Nana and Pop-Pop (Mouse) lived there. They were getting money and had a lot of the same things going on down there. Every day stuff, people out on the block, kids on the basketball court riding up and down the street on their bikes. The dope boys standing outside on the corner hanging around and police riding up and down the block cracking heads and walking in and out of the alley, hood fights and drive by shootings. Annapolis is a lot bigger than Pioneer City and about 15 minutes from each other. As soon as I would get inside of my Nana's house, I would run straight upstairs to my uncle Mar's room and put on his gold chains. I would look in the mirror and tell myself I'm going to get me some jewelry one day. He would just sit there and laugh and tell me, nephew you are crazy. I just knew I was going to have it all one day. I would always try and get him to let me wear his chain to school but he wouldn't do it. He told me to go to school to learn and I all I could do was respect that. Pop-Pop was always either playing the game or holding a dice game in the living room with his friends. They would have the whole house cloudy with smoke. I would go next door to see if Drop was home, so we could play some basketball. His father Papose and my Pop-Pop were best of friends and would always hang together before my Pop-Pop passed away.

I was always with my mom. My dad was around, but not as much as he should have been. He would come get me on the weekends and take me down to Newton 20. I loved it down there. It was like my second home. I even went to Rolling Knolls Elementary for a while down there. My father started to come me less and less. It bothered me at first because I would look forward to chilling with him in Annapolis. I always had fun every time I went down there. There was always something to do. I remember there was this big goodie bus that would pull up with all the snacks on it. I knew my dad was in the streets though. He had another family, my little brother and sister that he had to take care of too so I understood why I wasn't seeing him as much.

In the year 2000, I graduated from 5th grade at Van Bokkelen Elementary School. It was then that I knew my life would change. I was growing up and becoming more of a problem involved in the streets. I had already made up in my mind that I was going to be a drug dealer. The transition from elementary to middle school I knew was going to be a bumpy road; the school was bigger, the kids were older, and I was unsure of what was to come.

Before I end this chapter, I want to share with you how influential the people around you can be in your life whether good or bad. I became fascinated with the older guys making money fast and I knew that I was going to get it one day or another.

Childhood

2002-2006

I knew my life would change after elementary school because of the amount of exposure I had to real life things and situations. These things had an influence on the lifestyle I was headed towards. We were still living behind the front store in The Orchards. After graduating the 5th grade I started at Meade Middle School. My first day there was good. I knew most of the people there because they were either from Pioneer City, Providence or out of Laurel, Maryland. I rode the bus to school, but I never liked it because the kids were boring to me. I wanted to me around kids that were like me, always in the middle of everything and getting in trouble. My behavior started to change for the worse as I got older. I liked catching the bus that had all the girls on it, or I would walk down the street and catch the bus with the kids that were having fun on it. They would act crazy and give the bus aid a hard time. I felt like as a teenager there was a lot to prove from where I was from. I saw kids get chased home after getting off the bus, or getting stuff taken from them like snack money, CD players and iPods. You had to stand up for yourself if someone was picking on you and fight back whether you thought you were going to lose or win. You had to earn respect from the other kids by standing up like a man and not backing down. If you didn't stand up, you opened yourself up to people thinking they could take anything from you, including your freedom.

For some kids, school was one big popularity contest. It was all about being a class clown and making everybody laugh, showing up late and being disruptive, getting suspended or having in school detention. All of these things made you "cool" and made others want to hang around you so they could be "cool" too. It's crazy that some kids really thought those things were cool, when really all they did was make you look like a fool. Between in school detention and suspension, I was always getting either one at least twice a week. I had a good relationship with my administrator Ms. Slaughter who tried her best with me until the principle had to eventually put me out of the school for my behavior. Most of the time I would be at home because of being put out of school on suspension. I was hardly learning anything in school anyways. I stayed getting into some type of trouble and doing things I didn't have no business doing. Some days I would miss the school bus on purpose so that I could be late for school. I didn't want anyone giving me a ride either, so most days I would ride my bike or a couple of friends and I would walk and do dumb stuff on the way to school. We would throw rocks at cars or knock on somebody's door and run. We used to sit in the Subway or this place called Gianni's across the street from the school until they started calling the school on us. They would call the police to come escort us out of there but before the police showed up, we would run to 7/11 and steal some candy to take back to school and sell. I was having so much fun that I didn't even realize how quickly my first year slipped pass and I ended up failing the 6th grade and watching everybody else pass to the 7th grade. I felt so dumb and left out, which was expected since I played around and thought school was a joke. The only person to blame was myself since I couldn't get it together and focus my attention on what was important. I was constantly messing up in and out of school and getting in trouble with the police that eventually I ended up getting put out of Meade Middle School in the 7th grade. My mother ended up home schooling me the rest of the year, but she was getting tired of me and my behavior. The beatings weren't working anymore, and she didn't know what else to do. She eventually stopped calling my dad because he wasn't helping either. I was out of control and I was going to do what I wanted regardless of the consequences. I was so far gone that my mind was already made up to be in the streets. I didn't care about finishing school or anything for that matter. I was stuck in my ways and looking back it's sad that I treated my mother that way, but I never really had a father figure in my life to teach me what was right.

I tried playing basketball for AAU or JYPO. I was only going because my homeboys were trying out or playing for them, but I never followed through with it. I always ended up back on the corner hanging out. I feel like if I had a father like theirs that kept me in sports and showed me the right way, things might have turned out differently for me.

You never know where life will take you. I ended up moving to Annapolis in the Bywaters neighborhood with my friend Honeybun. Her children are my little cousins. I had a lot of fun down there. Everyone would be out on the strip all day and night playing dice games and just hanging out. People would run up to crack heads cars when they pulled up on the street. You had to be on point or you would miss your opportunity. The car wouldn't even get past the U-turn before somebody would start sprinting on feet to catch up with them. You weren't getting any money out there unless you already had your clientele on the phone because at least 5 to 10 people would be out there just waiting for cars to pull up. I remember my first time trying to sell drugs. I had gotten my first pack from down there and had no idea what I was doing. Only thing I knew was that you were supposed to hide it under your sack in case the police rode up, but I ended up dropping mine somewhere and I knew somebody had found it. I just had to chuck it up as a loss. My first time running to a car was with Fatboy, but Larry had us beat because as soon as I jumped on the sidewalk to run, I slipped in the grass on some dog crap.

Everybody was laughing, and I knew that chasing down cars was not for me.

In Bywaters I was hanging with all the hustlers and older dudes just like I did in Pioneer City. I was still cool with some dudes my age like Lil Bop and Whamp. They liked to pull all-nighters, but I couldn't get with it because I would be tired going to school the next morning. One day we were riding around in the green bean like 5 people deep hitting all the hoods. We drive through this one hood and they came running to the middle of the street and start shooting at the car. Somebody had put the car in neutral so when he pushed on the gas the car wasn't going anywhere. I was determined to make sure I didn't get hit by a bullet so me and Fatboy got under the seats in the back of the car. My boy Lil Short got out of the car and started shooting back. I will never forget that night, it was crazy and still to this day we laugh about it.

Meanwhile, my school setting had changed completely. I was no longer allowed to attend a regular school due to my behavior, so I was sent to an alternative program called Phoenix Center Academy in Annapolis. I knew a couple people from when I was younger growing up in Annapolis that attended already. The school was a different setting; the building was smaller; the classrooms were small and closed in with a small number of students in each room. There were two teachers in every classroom; I really didn't like it and I could hardly focus. There were fights like every other day, students would yell in the hallways and cuss the teachers out. The school started at elementary grade level and went all the way up to high school. The elementary kids were really bad and the food that was served to us was in aluminum foil. This school was for kids who got expelled from a regular school or had behavior problems and couldn't handle being in a classroom with a lot of other children. I hated it and tried so hard to get out of there. I ended up spending the rest of my 8th grade year there and then moved back with my mother.

I remember there would be days that I would be in the house playing the game and my cousin Los would come in the house with these trash bags filled up with something. One day when he went to the bathroom and shut the door I ran into the room and looked in the bags. I couldn't believe what I was seeing; there was so much money in those bags. Then I tripped over these shoes boxes that were on the floor and knots of money wrapped in rubber bands fell out of the boxes. I hurried and scooped all the money back into the shoe boxes and rand back in my room like I was playing the game the whole time. I couldn't stop thinking about where he got all that money from. I mean I barely seen him. He would come in and out of the house like once or twice a week. I had always heard about him though, about how he always had Pioneer City on lock and looked out for all the dudes out there. After I had discovered all that money, I went to school throwing up 20's, 10's and 5's everywhere. I felt like the man! The kids were scattering all over the hallway trying to grab the money that I was throwing. There was so much money I didn't know what to do with it all. If I would have known back then what I know now, I would have invested it. I got a huge rush seeing my cousin Los with thousands upon thousands of dollars, cash money. From the cars to the clothes and jewelry, the pictures from the clubs with bottles and half naked girls, I wanted the street life even more. I used to lay back on the bed with my hands behind my head telling myself that I was going to be just like my cousin Los one day. I'm going to get money and have all the things he had.

I will never forget this night and I still remember it like it was yesterday. We were all over my grandfather's house playing the PlayStation and my grandfather and 'dem were playing cards and gambling. My cousin Los had come by the house for a little bit to drop something off to my Uncle Tony and then left. They always said they had a funny feeling about the guy Los had around him, but I had never seen him for myself. I stayed over my grandfather's house that night so when I got up the next morning, I walked to my mother's house up the street. When I got to the house police were there and they wouldn't let anyone in. I didn't know what was going on, but I could see my mother sitting on the couch in the house crying. The police finally let me in and my mother immediately told me to go back to my grandfather's house. I didn't ask any questions; I just started walking back to his house. When I got there, the house was surrounded by family and people from the neighborhood. They said that Los had been set up and was killed. I couldn't believe it. I just sat on the couch in disbelief thinking about how my family told Los not to trust that guy. I never thought the night before would be my last time seeing Los. That incident changed my whole mindset about the street and not to trust anyone!

My mother had shirts made for my brothers and I because she didn't want us seeing everything that was going on at the funeral. We were all messed up about this incident for a while; there were so many different stories going around. People from around the way started acting and moving funny. They were popping up with new cars and packs, stuff they didn't have just a few months ago. After Los died, the hood went downhill; money wasn't flowing through there like it used to when he was around. There were still a select few people that were getting money, but they were very low key and laid back with it because of all the snitching that was going on around there. It's crazy how you could be getting money with someone you call your brother or friend that you would do anything for, and then end up becoming a state witness against them just to help yourself out. It all comes with the street life though; you sign yourself for some stuff you never knew would come with it. There are no rules in the streets and there definitely is no respect. The problem is there are no more old heads for the young boys to look up to. The old heads look like the young ones, so they have no respect for them. The streets need more older people like it used to have where the young boys had too much respect for them to act up.

Before I actually jumped into the streets, I used to hit up the malls with my little cousin Chubby/Taz. We started linking up with someone we knew working in FYE back when portable DVD players were popular. We had someone throwing them to us as long as we gave him a percentage off of each one we sold. We were selling them for like $50 apiece and we were selling at least 6 to 10 of them a day. This was my hustle. It was fun while it lasted since the guy ended up quitting before they could fire him. We were making some decent money off of hustling those DVD players, for being only 15/16 years old and no bills to pay. I always wanted to be able to get my own stuff without having to ask my mother or anybody else for anything. I used to get tired of walking up and down the street with no money in my pockets. I saved up enough money to buy some drugs and sell on the streets. I was moving too quick and being dumb because I just wanted money and I saw how easy it was to get in the streets. I was trying to be grown!

I bumped into this guy named Liq while walking down the street. I hadn't seen him in years before this. He was from Baltimore City but had moved down the street from me. We started back chilling together and I showed him the drugs I had and what I was trying to do with them. From that point on, I could say I was really deep in the streets; there was no turning back. A couple of us would post up on the strip, Pioneer Drive in the back of Creek Court. I would get most of my product off there and kick it with my homegirl Kee-Kee. I never bought my product where everyone else was getting there's from because we all couldn't be on the same block selling the same stuff or there would always be competition. I would bag my product up in some nice size bags and give out more to the crack heads so they would keep coming back and bring me more sales. I treated them nice like they were human and made sure they didn't feel less of themselves. Unlike other people, if the crack heads came to me with coins, I would still accept it. Most people wanted straight cash and the exact amount for whatever they were coming to purchase. We needed the crack heads just as much as they needed us. We were chasing that money and they were chasing that high.

I used to always hit dice games as well; that was another hustle of mine and I rarely lost. My everyday hobby after I got out of school was to drop my books off, hit the strip and get a couple of dollars. If the bikes were out, I might jump on the dirty bike and mess around in the street until the police start chasing me on it. I'll hit up the basketball court and shoot some ball until it was time for me to go in and get ready for school the next morning. Every day I would wake up and get ready to do it all over again. Some nights on the weekends I would stay out all night until the next morning chasing that dollar. I would use my grandfather's house as a get-away so that I could stay out all night on the corner. A couple of those late nights would pay off. It felt good to be able to school shop for myself and pay for my own clothes and shoes. My mother would get what she could for me but whatever she couldn't do, I would do for myself.

I started getting put in lock up for stuff I didn't have any business doing like; trespassing, disorderly conduct, grand theft auto, and assault. Once my name was out there the police would always harass me. They would jump me anywhere, sit me down on the curb and search me, slam me up and tell me that if they saw me outside again before their shift was over, they were going to lock me up. The police would accuse me for things other people were doing and try to put charges on me. They hated me and told me they couldn't wait until I turned eighteen so that I wouldn't be released to my mother anymore. I used to think it was cool getting locked up in front of everyone. I would hear them yelling, saying get off him, let him go, leave him alone; yall are dalways messing with somebody. The whole time I was making a fool of myself, not realizing that I was going to have to pay for my actions later down the road. I didn't think all this was going to catch up to me, but it did. I was in and out of the Boys Village/Cheltenham Placements (Youth Detention Center). I still didn't learn my lesson; it was all a joke to me. I knew I was going home one day and the police didn't like that fact that my mother would come down to the police station and get me. They were hoping that she would leave me in there so that they could take me to juvenile jail. I was out of control, so much so that the last time I got arrested my mother told me she was not coming to get me if I get locked up again. She told me I better call my father if I get in anymore trouble. They also called Juvenile Justice and gave them the green light to put me away and lock me up until my court date. I was there for a couple of months when I first got there. I ran into my man DC/Sizz during intake. He was from down 20 and was sent to Unit 6 while I went to Unit 8. I went to Placement but came home just in time to start my freshman year of high school in Pasadena.

Whoever is reading this I just want you to know that I learned a lot during this chapter of my life. I learned about crime and being in and out of jail. I lost friends and family members to money and violence. With all that was going on, I still managed to get my education and graduate. My education played a major role in my life and it will for you as well. I knew being in the streets was only going to be temporary so don't become fascinated with the fast money because it doesn't last long. Always put school first because your education is what's going to take you further in the long run.

Teen/Adulthood
2006-2018

Going into high school, I knew it was going to be a bit difficult for me since I'm a minority. I began my journey at Chesapeake High School. I was originally supposed to be at Meade Senior High, but I was still in the alternative program. The only good thing about the program was that it carried over into a regular high school. It was difficult at first having to adapt to a new school where I didn't know anyone. I wasn't allowed to attend Meade where all my friends were because of my past altercations in middle school. My past followed me from middle school and I was still paying for it. The Board of Education said they didn't see any improvement in my behavior to attend my regular school even though I did everything they asked me to do, it still didn't matter to them. I didn't let that discourage or stop me though. I was determined to get back to my home school. After a few weeks, I had gotten use to Chesapeake. It was made up of 90% white people and 10% African Americans. The alternative students had their own hallway and were sectioned off from the rest of the school. In order to make it to the main stream classes you had to have good behavior and no suspensions or referrals. The only time we really interacted with other students was in between classes or at lunch time.

I went 3 years straight without getting in trouble or giving anyone any problems. I wanted to go to Meade High so bad and I had a parent-teachers meeting before they decided to let me go. They discussed everything from my work ethic to my progress in behavior. I can honestly say that program helped me change a lot since middle school and I was definitely humbled through the process.

As I was getting up to leave the meeting, they asked me if I was ready to go back into a regular school setting and I shook my head yes. I really felt like I was ready, I wasn't the trouble-making class clown that I used to be anymore.

I started my senior year at Meade High School and it was such a great feeling! I couldn't believe I was actually at my home school now. There was so much love from everybody when I got there; they were definitely happy to see me back in school. The last time I had seen most of my homeboys and female friends was in the 7th grade. I just knew I wasn't going to last long there though.

All of my neighborhood friends and my middle brother, Duke, attended Meade together, so I knew we were ready to act up. There was a lot of animosity in the hallways amongst my neighborhood crew and the boys from Laurel that tried to fake like they were from DC, when really, they came from Russett and Maryland City. The neighborhood beef had been going on for years though.

School had started in August and I was put out in October for a fight that turned into a riot. My brother, some dudes from my neighborhood and myself were involved in a fight that broke out at the Arundel Mills Mall by the movie theatre over the weekend, and it carried over to school that Monday morning. My crew and I were talking about it outside before we walked into the cafeteria for breakfast and confronted the dude. He was sitting at the table and I walked up to him and said, "What's up? Y'all tried to jump my brother and them?" He tried to act like he didn't know what I was talking about. I was like right here, see him, 1-on-1, and after a little bit, it just escalated. I ran upstairs to the detention room where one of his homeboys was at and confronted him even though he had nothing to do with it. I just wanted to fight whoever, so I said what's up to him, he said what's good and I 'stole' him in the face right then and there. We get to fighting and I thought his homeboys were going to jump in since I approached him like that, but they just sat there and watched the whole time. I know if that was my homeboy fighting and someone was on top of him, I would have jumped in. The police came in the room and broke up the fight, but they only came after me; they slammed me on my face and locked me up. My brother and homeboys had been locked up and were already at the police station. The other guys wrote a statement about how we started the fight so none of them got locked up. I thought that I was going to get released because it was only a school fight but since I was 18, I was considered an adult. They booked me and made me sit in that dirty holding cell on a medal bunk and wait for hours before taking me down to Annapolis to the Commissioner. This was my first time being charged as an adult, so I didn't know how anything worked. There were people in front of me going up for whatever they had done; some went home, some got bails, and some were sent to the Annapolis Detention Center. When it was my turn to go up he, he went over my charges ended up setting my bail at $15,000. I looked at him like he was crazy, like are you serious. It was just a school fight.

I sat in my cell for like 3 days just thinking about how I messed up my whole senior year of high school. I didn't even tell me mother what happened, I figured my brother had said something to her when she picked him up from the police station. I knew I was going to have to hear her mouth, telling me this and that and how I never learn. It wouldn't be the first time she cussed me out. I had to get back to reality though because I didn't know if I was going to make bail or not. I hadn't talked to anyone, so I was unsure if they knew that I had a bail or how much it was. I had so many questions running through my head like whether or not I was getting out, if I would still be able to go to prom and if I was still going to graduate. I pretty much knew that I was not going to be allowed back at Meade High and they were going to send me back to Chesapeake High School. I couldn't believe I put myself in this position knowing I was supposed to graduate in a couple of months. My mind was all over the place, but then I heard the correctional officer pop open my cell door. I heard him call my name and I jumped off that bunk bed so fast. I couldn't wait to leave behind those nasty trays of food and juice they call base that they would use to clean the walls with. The officer said I had made bail and told me to pack up! I really didn't have anything to pack or take with me except my papers that told me what I was being charged with.

I was worried about getting back into school because I still had a chance to graduate and I didn't want to mess that up again. I ended up being suspended for ten days and until further notice. When they called my mother and I in for a meeting, they ended up taking the other guys side and expelled me from school for good. I didn't know what to do after hearing that I was put out of school. It wasn't fair to me how they went about the whole situation. Out of everyone that was involved, I was the only one that got expelled. Everyone else got to come back to school after their suspension was over. I was mad at first, but I eventually shook it off. I told myself that every time I see one of these dudes at any of the basketball or football games, I was going to punch one of them and they were going to feel my pain from be expelled. After two weeks of being out of school and not knowing what they were going to do with me, my mother finally took me down to the Board of Education and they said that I couldn't go to anymore public schools at all. I laughed at them like they were crazy. My principle from Chesapeake High, who I had a good relationship with, ended up calling the Board while we were in our meeting and pulled some strings for me. As soon as I had gotten out of jail, I called her and asked her to see if she could get me back into her school and before you knew it, she had me back up there. I was still going to court for the assault charge from the fight, but I finished the resto of my senior year at Chesapeake High and graduated on time. It felt surreal! I was just sitting in a jail cell trying to face reality and I managed to stay strong and keep my faith in God.

Now that I was finished with high school, I didn't know what I wanted to do. I was looking for a trade to get into, so I ended up giving Lincoln Tech a try. I took up HVAC, but I wasn't really feeling it. The recruiter kept pressuring me to sign up for it so that really why I went. I wasn't driving at the time, so I really didn't know how I was going to get there every day. It worked out for about two weeks. My homeboy Jack was going to Lincoln Tech for auto-mechanic and had the same schedule as me, so I just caught a ride with him since he lived in the court right before me. After a while, I just stopped going to school out of nowhere. I really gave up that easily and didn't even care about the loan I had taken out to pay for the school. I didn't have a job either, so in my eyes the only option left was to hustle. If I knew then what I know now, I would have finished my trade school.

I wasn't keeping up with my court dates because I was too busy running the streets and I ended up missing one. I was sitting outside one day just chilling when police rode up and jumped out on me saying that I had a warrant out for my arrest. I was confused at first but soon realized I had forgotten about my missed court date for the fight that happened at school a year prior. This time the commissioner gave me no bail and I sat in jail for sixty days until my next court date. They gave me time served for those sixty days that I sat waiting to go to court. I ended up taking a plea so that I could get out and get back to making money.

Before I got put out of Meade High, I was 'messing' with this girl who lived on the Fort Meade Military base. We had lost contact with each other after I got put out of school, but one day as I was getting ready to walk into the mall, I saw her and her homegirl. Her homegirl pulled me to the side and was like you know she's pregnant. I was immediately scared because I did not know what to do with a baby; I was still young myself. I wasn't sure who to tell, but a couple of months later, my son Armon was born. We had stayed in contact with each other after that day I seen her at the mall and I even went to the hospital a couple times to sit with her and see him. I couldn't believe I had a son. They ended up moving out of state for a couple of years after her father got orders to relocate. He was in the military and was being stationed somewhere else. She ended up going back to where she was from so she could be with family. That was hard for me to deal with because her and I were not on good terms, and my son was only a couple of months old when they left. I understand why she left and didn't say anything; she was so young and had the responsibility of raising a child and I hardly knew anything about being a father. I didn't want her to leave but she wasn't eighteen yet, so she didn't have a choice. Her sister ended up staying behind so I stayed in contact with my son's mother through her. I figured we would see each other again one day. I made sure not to lose contact with her this time, but I was unsure about when I would see my son again.

It was a rainy day and I had just gotten home from staying out the night before and I was bored. I decided to bring my dirt bike outside. I figured there weren't going to be any police out there this early in the morning. I had a lot on my mind after my son and his mother left and it took a few days for it to hit me. Anyways, I'm riding around all through Pioneer City, Meade Village and back over to Still

Meadows. I didn't know that I was riding dirty the whole time with drugs in my pocket. I didn't care if the police tried to stop me because I had already made up in my mind that I wasn't going to stop; they were going to have to catch me. I was coming down Pioneer Drive and I saw them coming up the street. I had a ski mask on, so they couldn't tell who it was, but it didn't matter because they knew what my bike looked like. They put their sirens on and I took off toward my house. I got up in my court and parked the bike in someone else's yard in case they tried to feel the engine to see if it was hot and say someone was riding the dirt bike. I already knew they were going to come to my house because they had taken bikes from out of my yard before. Anyways, I was leaving out of the neighbor's yard from stashing my drugs in their bushes and when I look up and turn around, the police were on me and the house was surrounded. The one officer that was always harassing me as a juvenile and looking me up just happened to be one of the officers that came behind the house. While they were back there searching, I tried to pull away and run in the house, forgetting that I had a crazy dog in there so of course the police came running behind me. Before I could stop my dog, she bit the police officer in his leg. We were tussling around to get out of the house and I was trying to tell the officer that I could get the dog off of him. I really was lying though. My dog didn't listen to nobody,

I just didn't want the officer to shoot her. He ended up shooting her twice anyways and killing her. I just knew she was hurt; I seen when the bullet hit her right in the side. My mom was really hurt by that because that was her favorite dog who she loved more than anything. She would even get the dog Chick-fil-A before she would get me anything. The dog was eating better than me in the house.

All the police ended up jumping on me and kneeing me in the neck and the head. They had found the stash in the back of the house and I just knew I wasn't coming home since I had violated my probation. At this point I just wanted to get to my cell, go to sleep and hope that this was all a dream. After laying on that cold ground in a puddle of water, they placed me back in front of the same commissioner. He gave me no bail and I sat in detention for 6 months going back and forth fighting this charge. I ended up having to do 18 months for my new charge and 18 months for violating probation from the charge I already had of intimidating a witness. I had to serve my time in the county, but it went by kind of fast. I knew everybody that was in there. I was on the same tier with Church and GMK; we all worked in the kitchen together. When it was nice outside, we would go out in the yard and hoop. After a couple of months, I was allowed to go to work release. My cousin had a shop, so he was able to pull me out on work release but it didn't last long at all.

One day I left the job and went to a cookout at Dorsey Park. Everyone was out there from all over the place and people thought I was home. I was still locked up, on work release, I had just snuck off the job before it was time to go back to the jail. Anyways, these girls ended up fighting and somehow my name got caught up in it. The girl's mother called the jail and told them that I was at the cookout fighting so I ended up catching a new charge while still incarcerated. They gave me a street charge at that, so when I went back to jail, they sent me straight to lock up. They ended up taking 30 good days from me which pushed my release date back. I was supposed to go home in April but I didn't get home until July.

When I came home, I went and got a job at the Honda Dealership to try and get on my feet. I wasn't really the type of person that could work for someone else because I wasn't good with rules or taking orders, but I actually liked this job. All I did was drive cars around from city to city and state to state and most of the people up there were cool. I met a couple of good people; my man, D-Skip, from the city out in Westport; my man, Rashard, from DC and my man, Chuck, from Columbia. We all had the same schedule and pretty much did what we wanted up there. After like two years of working there, I left the job.

I ended up having my second son, Amir. I had been trying to get with his mother since we were in school together. I finally seen her out one day and hooked up with her before I got locked up. She stayed by my side the whole time and when I came home, we got a crib together and had our son. I left my job so I could go back to the streets and this time the money was coming in fast. I had gotten tired of somebody telling me when to clock in and when to take a lunch break. I could do whatever I wanted, buy whatever I wanted and go wherever I wanted. Every other day my man Foo and I would ride up to Chevy Chase at Tyson's Corner and go to Norma's every weekend. My uncle, Teddy, Foo, Ms. Shani and I took a trip to Puerto Rico for a couple of days. It was two weeks later on May 23rd after we had gotten back that I received a phone call I did not want to hear.

"Hello."

"What's up?"

"Man, Teddy got set up and was killed."

I couldn't believe it! We were just sitting in his house chilling and talking about how he was getting ready to open a corner store. All I could think about was his family and his kids. It really didn't hit me until I seen him lying in that casket at his funeral.

After that, Dre, Foo and I went to Miami, Florida. Everybody was down there! We ran into a couple of good dudes from Annapolis, Whamp and Cash. When we came back, we had a little chill spot called the Apt that only us who hung around each

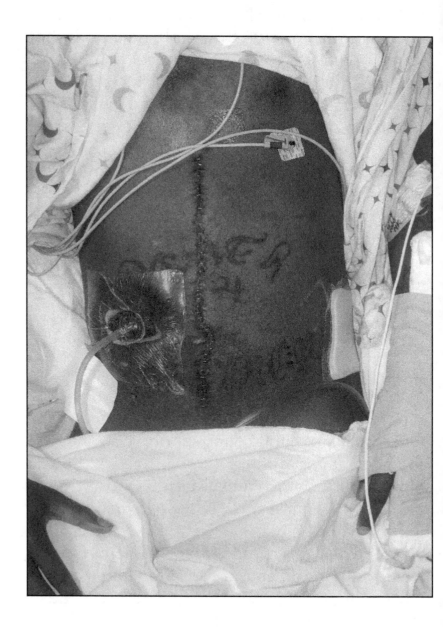

other every day would go to. One day I was sitting in my car thinking about what I wanted to do with all my money when I got a phone call from my barber reminding me about my appointment. CJ, also known as Clay Da Barber, was my Barber. He has been cutting my hair since I was a kid. I started telling him that I wanted to do something with my life. All I knew was the streets, but I wanted to invest my money in starting my own business. So, I brought up the idea to him about making my own clothing brand. I had second thoughts like everybody out here is trying to make a clothing line and plus I had no idea where to even start or what name to call it. Anyways, I started selling my shirts out of my car for a while and the business was growing.

I had a rough summer though. I had lost 2 good friends to the streets, Jokah and Drop. They were both good dudes with a lot of potential; young and getting money. After losing them, I got into a really bad dirt bike accident. We were all over Meade Village playing around on the dirt bikes and the police were coming down the street, so I took off in a hurry. I was going way too fast and when I turned into the court my back brakes stopped working. A little four-year-old girl was in my way, so it was either hit her or crash into a brick wall. I couldn't see myself running that girl over and taking her life, I would have never been able to live with myself for something like that.

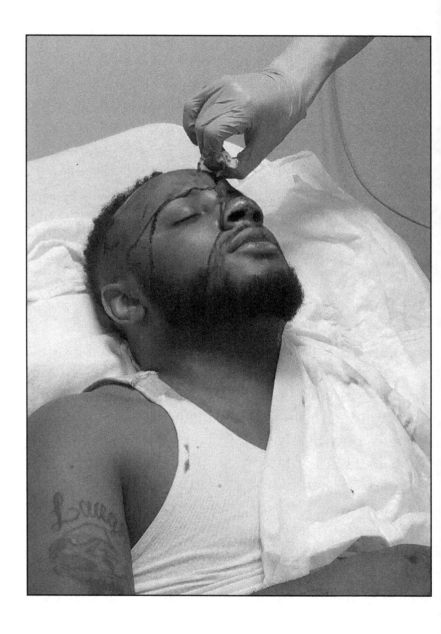

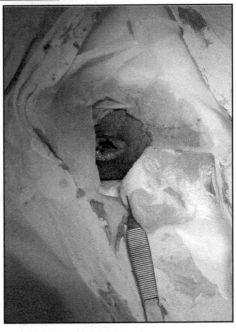

As I got closer and closer to her, I made the choice to sacrifice my life for hers and if it was my time to go then that must have been God's plan. I hit the green box and flew off of the bike face first into the wall. I jumped straight back up on my feet. I thought I was good because I didn't feel anything but then people were running up to me telling me I needed to go to the Emergency Room because I had a big hole in my head to the point where you could see some of my skull. I laid on the ground and waited for the ambulance to come but they were taking too long so a couple of people picked me up, put me in the car and drove me to the hospital. I told Slops to call my mother and tell her to have the doctors waiting when we pull up since she worked at the hospital that they were taking me to. I ended up leaving the same night with like 50 stitches in my head and face.

Five months had gone by and I was in the house playing with my son. I gave him a hug and a kiss and told him that I would see him later. I was heading to my grandfather's house over in Still Meadows and on the way there I couldn't stop thinking about how you should cherish people more because you never know when the last time you see them will be. I pulled up to my grandfather's house, went inside and took a quick nap. I went outside by the pool to check on something and was talking to my little man for a minute. After I finished taking care of what I needed to take care of, I was headed to

Annapolis. Before I was ready to leave, I seen this car pull into the court, but I didn't pay it no mind. I ran across the street to my homeboy's house to give him my gun until I came back since he was going to be outside chilling. I started walking up the street towards my car with my head down looking into my phone. I knew the same car that I had seen a few minutes ago was now following behind me slowly. As soon as I got to the stop sign to walk across the street, I picked my head up and it was too late. He was already out of the car with the gun to my chest. In the back of my mind I was like this can't be happening right now. This wasn't a dream. I was really standing there looking at a gun pointed straight at me. In a situation like this you have to think fast. Do I stand there? Should I run? The dude tells me to lay down and I said No! I would rather die standing on my two feet then to lay down. In that moment, I took off running. There was another dude in the car so before they could try and snatch me up, I pulled away and ran across the street. Next thing I hear is boom, boom, boom, boom, boom. I could hear the bullets flying past my head hitting the surrounding cars and fence. I felt the first bullet hit me in my back, then my shoulder and then my arm. I hurried up and hit the alley and ran up to the top of the court. I ran door to door trying to find someone to call the ambulance. I knocked on at least 4 doors before someone finally answered. My homegirl Dee Dee's

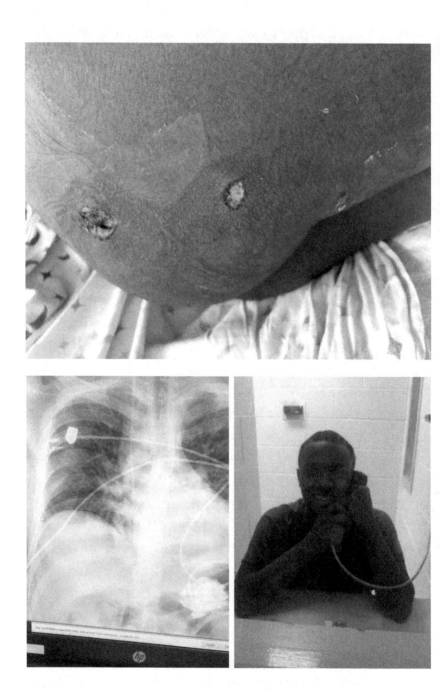

mother ended up coming outside and opening her door for me. She kept me calm and told me to lay down and try to relax while she called the ambulance for me. The first couple of times she called, she couldn't get through. Her youngest daughter was on her way to homecoming and she came downstairs crying and saying, Mama don't let him die. The thought of dying was definitely on my mind especially after losing two people from getting shot. I could start to feel myself losing my breath and shortly after that the paramedics came walking through the door. When they were pushing me out the door on the stretcher the whole court was lit up; everybody was out there. The first person I saw was my man Unk. The crazy thing is, he lives right by where it all happened, and I didn't run to his house first. I thought the paramedics were going to fly me to shock trauma, but they drove me all the way up there. My stomach was hurting the most and there was a lot of internal bleeding. There were doctors and nurses that filled the whole operation room up and they were trying to ask me where all I was hurting. I was trying to tell them my stomach, but before I could get it out, I threw up blood everywhere and that is the last thing I remembered before I passed out.

I woke up in a room with all these tubes hooked up to me. They were in my nose, my chest, and my mouth. I could barely open my eyes, but I could hear and feel the people talking to me. I couldn't talk because of all of the tubes so I would just nod my head. I was in and out of surgeries every day; I had at least 4 of them. I couldn't eat or poop for two weeks. I was miserable! I couldn't wait to go home and get in my own bed. I lost a lot of weight and I had to learn how to walk all over again.

Thanks for the help from my family and friends for being there every step of the way. They helped me get through every day I spent laying in that hospital bed. It took me a couple of months to get back on my feet as far as my health and strength was concerned. I did therapy to get my strength back in my legs and arms. I was still small, but I was drinking a lot of Ensure and Boost drinks to try and get my weight back up. As soon as I picked up some weight and got myself together, I was ready to get back to the money. I got pulled over by the drug task force. I knew somebody had put them on to my car when they said I did a roll and stop at the stop sign. They said they were informed that I was selling drugs out of my car. They pulled me out of my car without even asking if they could search it. Everything about my car was legal. I had my license, my registration and insurance. They didn't have a proper cause for pulling me over, but they found what they found in my car and locked me up. I knew they were just mad because the I wouldn't tell the detective that was on my shooting case who shot me. Every day he would come to the hospital and harass me about it. He took two

phones off of me the day that I got shot and was asking me who I was going to meet. One of the phones wasn't locked and there were messages in there about picking up money, dropping stuff off and asking how much you need and so on. Just off of that, he already knew what I was out there doing. Based off of the exchanged text messages I was sentenced to four years, all suspended but one year and a day prison time. I had to go through D.O.C in Baltimore City first. It was a big tall brown building like 7 stories high. There was about 9 of us shackled from our hands down to our feet, that they walked into the building. There were no steps in the building and if you had to go anywhere in the building, you had to be escorted on an elevator to every floor.

My first night there they didn't have any bed space available, so they put us all in a very small cell with no beds. We used the mats and sheets they gave us to sleep on the floor with until the next morning when a cell became available. I got sent to the 6th floor to Unit 6-B. The cells were small and there was already someone in there. He was waiting to get classified and he told me it could take up to 45 days to see case management, it all depends on who your case manager is. He was a cool dude who had been sentenced to 15 years. You lock in most of your time there until they ship you out to whatever prison they are going to send you to. I would just sit on my bunk, look out the window and think about how much I let my kids down by putting myself in a position to be locked away from them and having them ask where I'm at and why I'm not home.

Sometimes you could come out of your cell; depending on whether you were on the bottom tier or the top tier, they would rotate your rec time. You would be able to come out from like 8am to 11am and in between those times you were allowed to watch television or use the phone. After the time was up, you would be locked back in until 6pm of the next night. I sat there for 28 days before they transferred me to Baltimore City Correctional Center. BCCC was for inmates who were in minimum security and pre-release. There were two sides, the south side and the north side. I was on each side for a week until they shipped me to M.C.T.C, the new jail in Hagerstown, MD. That ride up the mountains was long and miserable. They put me straight on the compound in building 8 first and then they moved everyone around and sent me to building 5. Every time you would get moved you would have to wait up to 30 days to see a case manager. During that little bit of time I spent on the compound before they sent me up on the hill to pre-release, I seem some crazy stuff go down. People were getting stabbed; dudes were actually fighting over who's "girl" they were going to be. It was all crazy! I spent the rest of my time at Hagerstown and was sent home from there.

I came home and chilled for a couple of months trying to get things back in order. I was trying to pick up where I left off with my clothing line and figure out where to start again. I ended up starting this book that I'm writing now before I even got locked up and I decided to go to the library and type it up. I had gotten most of it done but I was tired, so I left to head home. There was nothing unfamiliar with where I usually park my car at down where I live. When I got out of my car I started walking with my head down texting in my phone. I looked up and seen this car parked the opposite way up the street. I knew all the cars that would park on the road I park on. As soon as I stepped on the side walk past the car and look up, somebody jumped out of the car with their hoodie tied tight so that I couldn't see their face. It was too late to even try and run. The first bullet, boom, hit me and blew my spine over the top of my butt bone. I kept trying to run but the other bullet, boom, hit me in my leg and I fell back holding my leg. It felt as though my leg was just hanging off, like it was barely attached to my body anymore. I fell to the ground and was sliding across the pavement with my phone in my hand. The next bullet, boom, hit me and went straight through my hand, knocking the phone out of my hand. The next one, boom, hit me in my stomach. After that my body went numb and I couldn't feel the rest of the bullets hit me. I thought I was done, like this was it for me. I thought once I fell to the ground, he was going to stand over top of me and finish me off, but he was shooting from a far distance. Once I seen him jump back in the car and pull off, I just laid on the ground for a while and tried to stay calm and relaxed. I had been through this before, so I already knew how to handle it. I could feel the blood pouring from my back and butt and I started playing with it. I guess maybe because the first time I got shot 2 years ago I had internal bleeding and didn't bleed out, so this time me bleeding out really bad was new to me. I could feel my flesh hanging out of my body, but I think I was angrier about having to go through the whole process in the hospital again. Being in the hospital unable to eat, experiencing needle after needle and surgery after surgery was not something I wanted to go through again. I was tired and just ready to give in and nobody came outside. I was on this little dark back road and thought I had seen my son walking towards me, but I was hallucinating. I could feel myself drifting away slowly but somehow, I told myself to get the phone and call the ambulance. I was lucky I had my other I-phone on me because the one he shot out of my hand had a hole in it and was split straight in half. I called my girl and told her that I had just been shot and to call the ambulance. I ended up calling the ambulance myself too and they told me they were in route as we spoke. Somebody that lived in the house that I was lying next to came out to help me and my girl was walking down the street towards me. She stayed with me until the paramedics showed up. She thought I had only been shot one time, because all she could see was the hole in my thigh. This time I was expecting to get airlifted by a helicopter to shock trauma but once again they drove me all the way there.

I knew this was going to be a long healing process again. This time I had gotten shot 9 times. I was on life support for a whole day, but I pulled through after having 6 surgeries. My lungs ended up collapsing from all the stress of having tubes all over my body, from my neck to my chest, my hip and my ribs. I was being fed through a tube and they had to attach my intestines back together. My mom would sit there all day with me to the point I would have to tell her to go home. I had to try and understand her perspective as a mother though. I know it was hard for her. I don't know any mother that wants to see her child dying or lying up in a hospital bed all shot up.

After a month in the hospital I finally went home and two months after that I found a bullet in my leg that I didn't know was there, but the hospital did. I was lying in bed chilling and I felt something hard in my leg, but I thought it was just a knot or something, so I didn't pay it no mind. A week went by and I felt the sane knot, but it was getting closer to my skin, so I decided to go to the hospital and get it x-rayed. Come to find out, it was a bullet and I had to have surgery for them to remove it.

My advice is to never let anyone know where you live and lay your head at night. Remember, everyone is not your friend, and everybody is not your bro. You never really know how a person you grow up around really feels about you. The love of money is the root of all evil and the hate is out here so watch out for the fake love. I hope that anyone that is headed down the same road I was, learns from my mistakes. The streets don't love you. They take you away from the people who really love and care about you, like your family.

Now is the time for me to start my new life. My old ways of doing things and former habits will not open up new doors for me. Everything I went through made me the man I am today. You have to go through the storm before you can appreciate the sunshine. I ask you God to help keep me stayed on this right path. My lesson in all of this is that I thought the fast life was the best life for me. People treat you like a celebrity when you reach a certain level in the streets but you also don't notice the people that envy you because most of the time same people that are showing you all the love, want your spot. Just because someone is beside you, doesn't mean they are with you. I tried to keep the hood motivated, but this was the thanks that I got in return. Now a days, they don't respect the truth. You don't notice who is really there for you until your life is on the line and friends and family are checking up on you. There is a difference! And with that being said, I still have a passion for the money, but now I desire to get it the right way. The point is, there is more than one way to hustle. You can't hustle in these streets forever because in this game, there is no loyalty. There are no friends; it's every man for himself. I learned that the hard way through my mistakes, but I'm glad I made it out of the hood to talk about it and hopefully help someone else. A lot of us are influenced by the negative image of the neighborhoods we live in and we represent these images. All it does is lead us to destruction; it's the sad truth, but it's the reality.

Now a days its all about popularity through social media and it's affecting us and the kids in our community. Be careful of the company you keep and the activities you involve yourself in. Why are you listening to them dudes hanging on the street corner that don't have your best interest at heart? When your parents are giving you advice or trying to tell you something, you should listen because they are telling you for a reason. Trust me, it is for your own good. They have been on this Earth a lot longer than you and they are trying to prevent you from making the same mistakes they did. They have seen it all, so just know when they are yelling at you or getting on you, they are just trying to help you out. Those dudes that you think are your boys aren't going to tell you what is good for you. All they are worried about is if you sold a pack for them. It all comes down to the money.

Never lock yourself out of your life opportunities! You have to push past all the opposition and know that there are opportunities out there for you. Don't ever give up, put your mind to whatever it is you want to do and apply the pressure. Don't ever stop trying! It would be foolish of you to continue making the wrong decisions. You are leading yourself down a path of destruction that just mind end in death. When you make the right decisions, you will feel so much better about yourself. Nobody said it was going to be easy out here, but no matter how hard it gets, you have to keep applying yourself. Keep striving for greatness and stay in school. Use those streets as classrooms to teach each other the right way to live. It doesn't make sense to grind all your life; just know that the life choices you make are ones you have to live with.

Helping others out is the best tool for you to be successful in life. If you are reading this, I appreciate your support. If you could take at least one thing away from this book to help you, then I feel like I have done my job. I want to invest in your life by sharing my experiences with you and giving you some knowledge about how to make better choices. I hope this book can help change mindsets and help free at least one of you. If I can save just one life, then I have reached my goal. I appreciate the time you took to read my story and I understand that my life was orchestrated by God. His hand of grace and mercy was upon my life so that I could be a testimony of His greatness. It is my duty to give this information to those that are heading down the lifestyle that I once lived.

Closing/Last Remarks

I sold drugs because it was a gateway to most of my problems. Selling drugs will have you constantly in a state of worry. You will worry about people wanting to rob you all the time or worry about someone trying to end your life because they envy what you have. You will worry about the police and all the negativity around you. There is so much that comes with this lifestyle. It's a risky life to lead. Yes, I made money in the streets and I had a lot of good times, but sooner or later the consequences to all the poor choices I had made, caught up to me. I thought I was different, but I'm not. Most people don't make it very far in the streets. Some people lose family members, friends and even their own life. All of that can change if you just believe in yourself and move in a positive direction. God created us for a purpose and it's up to you to find out what your purpose is. Who are you? Find yourself! I'm just trying to save a mother, father, brother, sister...from going through an experience my family had to go through. Think before you act. Don't get put in a situation you don't have any control of. Have fun as a youth; you don't want to rush into adulthood. I'm writing this book today to reach out to the youth so that we can break the cycle.

My advice for you is to strive to make the right choices and be a positive influence in your neighborhood and community. Be a role model for the generations behind you. Learn from my mistakes and from others as well. Don't glorify the street life because it is just a dead end at the end of the road. Some people make it out and some people don't, but it's not a game you can just turn off. The only thing you get out of this game is a small cell or a casket. The streets will leave you with two things: resting in peace or resting in prison. I really just want you to understand what you are signing yourself up for. The odds will always be against you. When it comes to the system fighting for your life, you will be fighting for yourself.

People will say they are with you but when push comes to shove the phone calls will stop, the visits will decrease, and the money will stop being sent. All of that will eventually fade away, leaving you with your choices and some hurt feelings. So, ask yourself this: Is this the life you really want to live?

CPSIA information can be obtained
at www.ICGtesting.com
Printed in the USA
LVHW080051130220
646732LV00017B/252